Also by Marie Ponsot

ADMIT
IMPEDIMENT

ADMIT
IMPEDIMENT

POEMS BY

MARIE PONSOT

ALFRED A. KNOPF   NEW YORK   1981

THIS IS A BORZOI BOOK
PUBLISHED BY ALFRED A. KNOPF, INC.

Copyright © 1958, 1960, 1964, 1977, 1979, 1980, 1981
by Marie Ponsot

"Hommages à Charles Perrault" and "Garden: Paeonia
'Souvenir de Maxine Cornu' " were originally published in
Poetry. Other poems in this book have been previously
published in America, The Little Magazine, Open Places,
Phoenix, Shenandoah, A Shout in the Street, Woman Poet:
Northeast, and Women's Studies.

Library of Congress Cataloging in Publication Data
Ponsot, Marie. Admit impediment.
(Knopf poetry series; 5)
I. Title. II. Series.
PS3531.049A64 1981   811'.54   80-2727
ISBN 0-394-51450-5   AACR2
ISBN 0-394-74845-X (pbk.)

Manufactured in the United States of America
First Edition

FOR

Mary Denver Candee
Marie Candee Birmingham
Monique Ponsot Rudnytsky
Tara Rudnytsky
Deborah Ponsot
Danielle Ponsot

Let me not to the marriage of true minds
Admit impediments . . .

WILLIAM SHAKESPEARE

CONTENTS

~
This symbol indicates space between sections of a poem
wherever such spaces are not apparent due to page breaks.

ADMIT IMPEDIMENT

FOR A DIVORCE

1

Death is the price of life.
Lives change places.
            Asked why
we ever married, I smile
and mention the arbitrary fierce
glance of the working artist
that blazed sometimes in your face

but can't picture it;

I do recall (1) shoes you left
in my closet, echoing worn-out
Gauguin; (2) how once under down
drugs I roared at you Liar! oh liar!
exulting in not lying
                ((as if
I'd made a telltale drawing . . .)

2

How dear how undark appear the simple
apparently simple wishes of the untried will;
how dark it is here and how
suddenly too still.

3

Glad I need not chance again
against your prone packed weight
my uncertain stance,
I giddy with relief
relax into mobility.

The state we made of love
that you fled out of,
empty-handed,
I have enlarged
into a new mainland geography
where I move as if unburdened where
my burdens bear me.
You said once I had
taught you human speech.
I am glad
I never taught you to dance.

4

Or, perhaps I drove you to flight.
Perhaps (freckled) islanded
I (skinny) was Circe;
Aiaia sounds familiar and
even on my crystal sands even
under my fragrant trees you
were a pig

a pig, and I a Circe stupefied who
could not tell the master from the man,
tusk-torn because too slow to know
I had in choosing you

dismissed Odysseus
and the luck of Odysseus and
his mind immune to magic
~

for a prentice hand the sea could tame,
a poor sailor, lotus changeling, destined
never to come home.

. . . or so let me flatter myself,
fabulously.

5

But if the fable go that way, it goes on,
to say that in myths gross beasts must
wound; it is their work; by this work
mere moon-starred magicians may turn in
to useful plainer day's-eye citizens
                    and so, that blind
                    boar whose tusks wound
                    becomes a cruel kind
of guide or christ, an unwilling
savior, greedy to the hurt that,
necessary, healed to a shiny scar,
serves to teach
identify or save.
And should this be the case
I wish I could say I'd rendered you such grace.

6

                    (. . . a drawing telltale
& pure as one of yours when you drew edged
objects—a bird, a wheel—in the shift
of the light they turn in; as you drew
the soft unpierced air that bore

sounds of wings and waters at Banyuls
where we sunstruck went up under the arch
where we came upon fountains))
                    and now
exactly I do
darkly I do
            recall the you of then when
every time you touched me it was true.

7

Deaths except for amoeba articulate
life into lives, separate, named, new.
Not all sworn faith dies. Ours did.
(1) I am now what I now do.
(2) Then in me
that stunning lover
                    was you.

NEW YORK:
APPENDIX OF PREDECESSORS

I

People, I offer all my options, see,
Sweepstakes tickets, wishbones, beans, boxtop offers,
Ranked by threes in rows of three

A lifetime collection,
Everything I've got,
Take the whole lot

And grant one wish
Preceded by a general please: Please,

Everyone stop dying
Just for a while a week do not
Rattle, throat sick of speech; bang
Steady, pulse thready and thinning;
Bullets, sleep in the chamber;
Accidents, be righted; infants, insist,
Accept the running blaze of breath
For now. Patience, Death.

Grant relicts this, give us ellipsis,
Time to count heads, catch up,
Or! if a week's too long wait just
An instant, stay, all stay;

Let the lately dead complete their exits;
Let me for once mourn well the
Stop of unstopped body as the person disassociates
And we are left to burn or bury what we can.

2

Born abed,
Bedded wedded,
Dead in bed;
We at any wakes and weddings weep it with
The one kind of tears; absurd they replace
All we have lost of the old charms; our one
Remaining Woman's Tabu: the Wedding Warning:
We use such tears to convey;
So to weep stuns.

Wakes are the worst weeping though.

O my blood.
Does nothing ever die.
Body more than body
Does no body ever die.

I watch over this disembodied body.
I learn how the new dead lie.
Wakes are ceremony, crazed.
Grief is an elemental air
The ungrieved cannot breathe.
So dumb is sympathy. The shocked
Stand to stupefy all comers who stare
No wonder like runners
Of long long hills
Whose, Sorry for your trouble,
Is a gasp like swallowed laughter
And the answer's desperate.

3

My father a man gave
A great shout and
Rearing up died.

Unfair, Pelican, o most
Unpitying to hurry so
To be unoccupied.

No fault of his. Mind,
I'm not ungrateful. Now
I'm landed gentry just like him.
He left me
Everything:
A strong box; a jest book
A sketch book and especially
Unfashionably a fat book
Of tender memories, all three
Mint, in boards, unfoxed, indeed
Unread, he is so dead.
In the box, securities,
Gilt-edged; some golden deeds;
And one note of hand owning
His wealth to be ambiguous,
An appendix to the fat book
Of predecessors he died debtor to,
Whose elegies yet to be written
He intended to have set
In granite when he got the time.

        What, friend! fresh out of time?
        Here, here's some of mine.

Your heir, I can give
What you cannot refuse or take,
A privilege of those who live.
Let me reckon up
What I may recuperate.

4

Cut a first stone.
Cut, for my father's Edwardian father,
Whose son 8 years old at 8 a.m.
Found him gorgeously asprawl
Inverse like Peter, resplendent in
Aureoles of haemorrhage, arms & coat
Flung open backward down the brownstone stairs:
       Jack Birmingham, young John that was,
       Invented for redemption
       The coupon label; his estate
       Includes 2 gross of mandolins,
       3 of ukeleles, and some mixed
       American premium guitars;
       Jack, who gambled for sons
       On a bride small-boned but arrogant,
       Whose gamble paid off in thirteen children
       Of whom three survived, one a son.
Nothing now no one will do justice
To enterprise, hard wit, fast choice,
A life lived laughing urging his pockets
To pleasure in big engraved cash dollars,
Though in his son my father's book I read
What years his hopes despaired on waking,

Knowing his father would not say again
The sentences he must have bubbled hot to no ear
Hung head down, into his fur coat collar,
Trying to make time teach us
How to say our morning prayers.

5

Old Calvary the Cemetery holds,
Among his parents grand and great
And the many small white boxes, his bones.
Aunt Dannie saw to it (Anne, not Danielle,
Daughter of Michael a hero
Of the fiery City, Brooklyn,
An honorary everything Volunteer), Anne
The shirt-waisted maiden, tortoise-
Shell combs in folded redgold hair, First
Woman Buyer for Stern's Department Store,
And never missed a day not even the day
They buried him her brother very decently
According to arrangements she had made.
It says here she deserved
A hill-capping Parthenon
But had no taste for thanks.

6

Kate comforted.
Kate (Katie to no one but the dead,
A sister, a second at most mourner)
Shawled the pain-stiff widow in a chair;
Tied the girls' ribbons and made the boys dress warm,

Admired snowmen often after school
Until evening, that bitter year,
Then called the children in, shook
Ashes down to bring the flames up,
Poured rounds of cocoa hot,
Counted them by name like kingdoms
Saying, "Mary how lucky you are, all
Within and none without, my dear!"

7

Summers came, one to memorialize Great
Uncle Jake (who south for the gone war
Fell, woke in a true clement meadow,
Became a Kentucky cooper taking unto him
A Kentucky beauty tall and lame); he
Many decades at peace came
Home to them with August
Walked across the bridge to Brooklyn
And invested in presents of ice cream sodas
Himself carrying vanilla and chocolate metal
Pails of them & trailing a ten-year-old boy
Who never forgot that hot afternoon
Up Berry Street striding, both hands tense
On the thin handle of a brimming strawberry third.
Jake took what a man with a niece can,
Pride, in gay-as-silks Mary perched
Neat, bright, unwinged on her rocker,
Her body brittle with arthritis and loss,
More broken than his mare-tossed wife's,
Her wide mouth between bites of pain

Calling her children to her
With jokes, promises of paradise,
Nonsense, and words to the wise.

Needing their love
A woman not fond
Not gifted with a mother tongue,
She learned to entertain,
Determined to see the girls grown
And her one son place his stakes forever
Outside that house of women
On a woman of his own.
(Mother, that was you, that girl
Then twelve to be for twelve years courted.)
Upon hearing that I
His child was born, Mary
Clapped her hands and flew
Entirely out of time.

8

Blurred generations of women,
Our expent medians, you leave us
In confusion in your debt.
We ignore of you woman
For woman why you were not witless
Half your hearts with all your dead
And half vicarious, attendant
On the triumphs of the live.
Groggy with joy and grief,
Infirm, analphabet, allowed for,

How was it you held steady
Without franchise where you stood
At the last extremity of love?
That house of women thrived on watching
Wishing pretty Rettie well, as she alone
Became a real turn-of-the-century girl,
Typist, teacher, lively, perhaps
Too intense. Home she came
Through downtown traffic, humming,
In a carriage hired by her last school
After something slick as birds
Splitting the air flew beaked
Through her and her racing heart.
Twenty, "I'm going to die, why not
Like this," she sang waltzing
Alone to the tune like her The Beautiful
Blue Danube too sweet too brief unripe
Rushing to a dizzied close.
One New York noon she put on gloves
Hat and veil, humming, and strode
Uphill to St. Someone's Gothic pile
And died,
That way, why not.

9

They tried
To remember her, what a soft lot
They were, copying out of love
Her light-catching wit, and what
They caught of it was her dire joy

Transparent to certain pain.
Kate the comforter at dusk for her
Went sometimes to the unblinded window
Saying softly, "Hark!"   Even
Thirty years later, delirious, her hips
Broken falling into what children
Fear, the cellar dark, Kate
Laughed like a girl, in a girl's
Unshaken voice cried plainly, "Rettie!
Oh! what fun." So Kate died,
Comforted.

10

Dead man, I cannot read your note of hand.
I cannot remember every anything you said.
So this anecdotal tree must stand
Gut-rooted, stemmed in the breast,
And branched in the brain and hand
To arbor honest grief
Until grief dies to understand
(As superstitions—like rock to sand—
Rot into the bottom soil of true belief)
How I am your triumph as phoenix
Whom I weep as pelican.

BASIC SKILLS

Crazy chopped shrieks of school
people penned in the scarred
yard stop at the metal
whistle blown hard.

Exposed among monitors, at
angles marked on the cement,
the children shrink. Teaching
screaming & cringing, the raw
teacher screams above
a selected 8-year-old boy.

What's outside the shiny
web fence is invisible,
unofficial, its random strengths
—natural hugs, curious energy,
all that only age of gold—
for these lead-alchemic hours gone
into the jailsteel boundary
taken in & glinting
like tears behind eyes he shuts, as
the head of the boy goes down.

DE RELIGIONE
HUMANITATIS VERA

> Hear us,
God of man's desire and will;
Maker and magnet, be near us
Who again plan to kill.

Lord of Man Destroyer of Man
Lord Slaughter we confess you
Our lives exalt your cause.

We adore you, o best, and we bless you.
Behold: with our precious gifts
We reinforce your word.
Deign to receive them:
> energy; passion; treasure;
> these persons to priest you:
> our dearest well-grown boys.
Sworn dying or killing to pleasure you
They vow to propagate your joys.

Rapt, enrapt with power, a far-darting
Light-swift, phantom-borne host, they
Lift up skill-hallowed hands:
> Maker of peace,
High priest and first principle,
Instruct them that their hands may
Worthily bestow you on those
We have chosen for you today.

We are yours, Lord War; you know it.
Shaped to your image our hearts
Are open to you, and open

The works of our days.
No matter what we have written,
What other gods we may praise,
We celebrate no mystery
But yours; it is your law we obey.
Our dreams, our doings, and our history
Witness you. Wherefore we pray:

Let the killer priests of our killer race
Go forth like justice blind to the kill
According to your will.

Let the rite of ruin prove
What our hearts ripe
For ruin believe.
O Father of Nations,
Gladly we perceive
Your glory performed:
Our acts of worship recreate
The substance of the archetype
In our own idiom. We elevate
        the failure of the woman
        who with her single body
        is trying to safesurround
        her several children; nearby
        intact with agony an old
        man sits on the ground
                our gentle sons
        have blasted in your name;
        they return to blast it again.

~

The skin of the children like peach
Skin splits and the fine flesh is
Giving us joy in you as we
Give them you, Lord Death.

This fresh decade of children
Takes shock of us; our skilled sons
See to it; they shock infants,
Innocence, local ignorance,
Into the perpetual
Newness of your ritual.

What they do is the best we can.
Their worship is ours, God of the Race of Man.

We offer the blood of their and our priests,
The blood of those the priests represent,
Lifeblood, theirs and ours. Better,
We who desire the spilling thereof
Offer our desire, our world's will bent
On becoming as your instrument
In the spilling of blood
As with garments of radiance, undulant,
With garments of sheer fire,
Our sons clothe the live children.

We exult as our sons become
According to the ardor of these acts
Your men forever, having sunk in you

The roots of their manhood, Lord Slaughter,
Their love for you absolute,
Once done all done,
Your servants henceforth, Lord War,
In whom
        all men are one.

THE ALIEN EXAMINERS

"Here is a rational
  beast agile at the thumb
  ignorant, concupiscent,
  and steeped in lethargy.

"Here is a he of the kind
  which casts up institutions
  that they pollute & cast down;
  more plentiful than pebbles,
  more complex, these fabrications
  are all based on two or three
  nightmares of the family.

"Note the sight apparatus: predictable
  organically apparently nothing new.
  But if we examine the retina
  we find non-repeating patterns,
  unique ones, like fingerscrolls;
  we find no two alike! Therefore no two
  samples see the same, as when they touch
  no two samples sense the same.
  Infinite difference! Wonderful.

"Ask him what he sees.
  He is not necessarily dumb.
  Most have a kind of language

they jump in & out of, to hide
as well as to keep facial muscles
supple for food intake. Sounds
they hear often they may repeat. Ask."

"What do you see?"
        "You've got me ass-up, mates.
        I'd answer better on my own two feet."

RESIDUAL PARALYSIS

for June Jordan

I'm an unable woman who loves to dance
but my polio leg won't go, or will
a while, until yanked by muscle cramps
that grip the ankle so it gives way
& locks twisted, perpendicular. And then
of course the damned thing's sprained, fat, blue, & wrong.

When I hear music I think nothing's wrong
that I can't manage, and I start to dance,
inside at first, smiling for the beat; then
the sound strides up my back & claims it will,
if I let it, float me safe all the way
on the long waves of high style nothing cramps.

So I'm a chump, surprised, betrayed by cramps,
ashamed to admit I have something wrong
until it's too late & rhythm drains away.
Let drop, I fall untuned outside the dance
insulted in the body of the will
to hold control, that cooled my fever then.

That I was sick, I kept half secret then.
Years of vanity, vain practice, vain cramps
got me walking even downstairs at will.
I valued that, my false claim, "Nothing's wrong!
(I can't press down a clutch and I can't dance
but) I'm not lame (not very, anyway)."

Lies have small voice where dancing has its way;
old true tales sweeten into the now of then
which is the breathing beat of every dance;

the wrecks & twists of history uncramp
into trust that present kindness can't go wrong
among warm partners of a common will.

I try. If I can stop lying, I will.
I'll claim my cramps & limit them that way,
trust & forget my history, right & wrong,
while others dance. I might, less vain than then,
forgive dead muscles & relax their cramps.
I can love dancing from outside the dance.

When trust uncramps the ordinary will
to laugh its way past accidental wrong,
those outside then step inside the dance.

SONG, FROM THEOPHRASTUS

Struggle makes its own strict sense.
The will kept sharp keeps free,
Learns reflex skill, cuts out pretense
    (the eye in the reed, the joint in the vine,
     the knot in the tree)
Dark evidence beneath the bark
Stars the wood where the heavily
Fruited branches rose and left a mark
    (the eye in the reed, the joint in the vine,
     the knot in the tree)
The thick-rimmed notch sustains
Grapes lustering toward wine
To bear the beat and weight of rains
    (the knot in the tree, the eye in the reed,
     the joint in the vine)
Rushes raise up a thread-spined length
In the union of their thrust toward seed,
Rooted and grounded in flimsy strength
    (the joint in the vine, the knot in the tree,
     the eye in the reed)
Bones unbroken lack the core,
The doubled strength of bones that be
Knitted to themselves once more
    (the eye in the reed, the joint in the vine,
     the knot in the tree)

ABOUT MY BIRTHDAY

I'd like to assume,
from my April birthday,
I quickened the womb
on the 4th of July.

If you suffered as I
a sternly fought tendency
to endless dependency
you'd know why.

SCRIPT FOR A HOME MOVIE
of the first Joyce Symposium, Dublin

I reeling with labyrinthitis from the tricks
of a new zoom super-8 was trying to disc
—over over & over (peep. tip.) Dublin
at the dearest Joyce Symposium composed
of June Jimlovers, scholar gossips,
boilers of his holy bones . . .

& here they are, at UCD, a lecture hall,
a lecturer, singing "The Lass of Antrim."
Here's some rubble, smallfar; zap
BIGTALL a half downed façade saying: 7,
under wallpaper flowers paling flapping;
and a dropback presenting
elegant Eccles Street still foursquare.

Here I'd a midwife companion (Oxon.). See her
bagbearing half a mile off on Sandymount Strand
AND GULLS TAKE TO
SIDESLICING FLIGHT FOR HER TOSSING THEIR
NAMINGS OF AIR down & up with Howth distant; pan,
to the right's the rim of, & here close it's the

Martello Tower! a circle of sun, stone-ringed;
the generous head bent to listen is FRANK
Budgen & the gentle lady of him KIND IN
CONVERSE with American academics; look beyond
now upSURGING Giorgio bursts german-
speaking out of the Stephenhole joining
them JOYCEAN WITH (o the image of his father,
accdg to Mz Veyl) his cheerful snarl graven
~

as against the plashsoft sky heads turn to watch
(pan) where among rocks among seachurn 3 boys
run to dive, dive,
                    dive
                        in.
Here the spacespoil
zoomer dizzied me, here
hackles rose on those atop
the tower   among whom then
                                was heard
                                the last
laugh from the live haunt of him
whose known to be transalpine bones
do not keep him from these stones
he shaped to build our Babel from.
Now too my
hackles rise
reviewing his projected shadow thrown
MENE on my wall to show
faint stains of intellectual abuse.
Well
PENANCE for imprudence
for having had the effrontery to
use a long booklove as excuse:
I go to black to do.

BILINGUAL

Languages before they are words
or systems are persons speaking
and persons spoken to. The bilingual
cannot, for example, convey in English,
"Au placard, la lavande
fait bien blanchir les linges";
there's no American woman to whom
it could be said.

The pain of having two languages comes from a
straining between them in the mind,
from a need to keep them separate and
a desire, forbidden, dangerous,
to marry them: like twins who
safely unentwined by each other's presence
stress their differences
and who when absent cannot but represent
longing for union of the purest kind.

The two tongues must be untrue to each other.
Their speaker always has one mute mouth kept pressed
closed against the barrier and already possessed
of other words to word each word better,
that the speaking one is deaf to.

Dreams give relief but no rest.
Both babble there, each other's audience,
making love eloquent at last, coupling
with the rich attention grand passion
gives in slowness to the body of the lover;
there the American answers, with pleasure,
"I love the smell of lavender."

FAITHFUL

always on the job, dependable
I am, like you, a burden bearer;
I comfort you, you comfort me.
steady on, brother ass!
look   our encounter
(so plain we don't believe in it)
sustains us as we plod heavily
far apart, not where we'd thought to be
not knowing my labor strengthens you
not knowing your labor strengthens me.
we see our comfort does not stale or tempt
us to quit, grab the chance, & flee.
maybe they meet deepest who must work to see
maybe we do believe, if secretly

your wild self/your wisewoman/your frien
I too keep a skinned grip on this minute a
watch out!
a sweet slick beast, solo
darts out from between our hand
flashes upward strongly
toward the ground of our great longin
where it runs free
timelessly
if we love the grip
or time or tra
we feel fre
if we love the trap enough
we leap free.

Dear my companion
never to be   let the sweet beast
keep free

"SOIS SAGE Ô MA DOULEUR"

I

Here they are, what you hid,
what shamed you, the
secrets of your life in cardboard
cartons at my feet (your
life you laid no claim to)
gifts, accomplishments, genius,
and what you did with these.

Here is the cast-off evidence,
amassed, earned, dry—
I read aghast through thousands
of pages of claims
you earned and hid and
did not choose to make
or did not make
or, no one heard you make

    while you made
dinner, jokes, love, kids'
tuition money, friends, the most
of dim situations,
and the best of everything.

You are extreme, being you & dead,
your beginning & end extremely visible;
but the dereliction of your crowded cartons
many women know
(and some men
who live like younger
sons or girls or saints—
but most who expect nothing
for work well done

31

are women) especially
women of my generation
—almost famous almost exemplary
almost doctors almost presidents almost
powerful, women entirely
remarkable, entirely unremarked,
             women with dues paid
             who lay no claim to what they've paid for
             and are ashamed
             to be ashamed to lay a claim.

I cry telling a woman (like you but
like me still alive, taking that chance)
of your secret works and unbanked treasury.
Redfaced I blow my nose & we
exchange stares her face stripped by insight
back from forty to fourteen; she knows;
the rose-petal peony of her snaps in a
jump-cut back to a bud, she looks
bud-tight, slices of white petal showing,
slowest to open where there is no sun;
there is no sun; our secret is your secret;
we see what we have done.
We see your life. It hurts us.
It is our life. There are many like us.
We have daughters; they have daughters.
What are we to do?   Many
and many like us would mock us if they knew
that we who mistrust power & will not compete for it
conceive of other claims but only in pain conceive
that we might make them.
~

. . . died at fifty. Is fifty young?
It is young. You died too young.
Dead woman, this side of despair
where I use you to say I care,
does knowing what we can't help
help? or was the absence of answer
fatal, was that the infarction
that sprung your heart apart?
did the infected heart, healed, fall loose again helpless,
did our helplessness prevent your breath
as you lay in wait for the too-late ambulance
until you drew an answer for us with your death?

What model did we who are like you give you?
none. One of us, as good as you a scholar,
worships to complete her late husband's opera; one
slips hand to mouth modestly and paints
essential paintings, goes on painting, who
sees it? only a few; as for me I start out
but everything I encourage to happen
keeps me from finishing

I do not write your name here
because it would hurt me;
you would have hated it; you deserve
silence for failure who had
silence for your excellence.
You had got used to that, made each success
a smaller plant in a smaller garden with less light,
and concealed among its leaves the stalks of suffering
perfectly unbudded, the sleekest secret.
~

Oh, no one discouraged you; many loved you,
everyone liked you, why not, so generous, oh the
parties; some did blame you obscurely: why
were you—gifted, rich—not famous?
That echoed in you,
didn't it; hurt your heart;
made your breath shorten with anxious guilt.

Step by step your breathless death accuses us.
The cartons found in your attic
full of your successful procedures
accuse us whose products are like yours
kept left-handed, womanly secondary
according to the rules. Whose rules?
How can we keep our hot
hatred of power
from chilling into impotence? You
could have disbarred the rules if anyone
had noticed you in time behind them.
With your costly help can we undo
the rules and with or without shame
lay our claims?
Should we who can be happy picturing
who we are, burst alive out of that frame
in our daughters' names?
I say
I am too old, tired, crazy, cold—to
say nothing of ashamed—
to try.
At my feet
your insistent cartons, their danger

implicit, speak or sing in
tongues or invisible flames.

2

Q: Brought to book at last,
     what did you say on your day
     after death, how did you
     sum up your argument?

A: This far side of dying there is no time
     for distance, and so no irony.
          I had to be plain; I said:
I was not a success.
I buried my treasures and lost the maps,
stewardess of my obscurity.
My life was comfortable, easy;
I was lucky; my one triumph was
to experience the world as holy
and to find that humorous.

I was beautiful by strict standards
for each age; dressed well, moved well.
I did not use my beauty.
I liked to be sexual; was shy until
I gave a good partner the pleasure
of teaching me. I made no capital of sex.

I was a wife, supportive, cordial, a helpmeet
and ornament; bore healthy children, mothered
them, improvised; entertained in-laws

as god-sent; kept up our correspondence;
was a presentable hostess, a lab-sharp cook,
a welcomer. Gratefully oh gratefully
I found I was married to a friend.

I came to terms with my family inheritance,
all of it; it did not merit me anything.
I loved my brother. I saw my friends.

I was a good student; women professors
dying left me their libraries & lonely valuables;
played Chopin when asked & Rameau when alone;
had ideas; did not turn intelligence into power.

I liked parties; liked drinks with one friend,
listening; celebrated epiphany; when I was ill
the interns took coffee breaks at my bedside
& told me their specialties;
I submitted to remedy.

Indoors my amaryllis rose yearly in crowds of flowers.
Blue gentians grew outside my country house,
and arbutus fragrant in early spring.
In my last years I watched the coming
and going, predictable & predictably
full of surprises, of birds
on the east-coast flyway. I understood
that they came & went of necessity yet
unaccountably, in mixed flocks, in their
various plumage, unaccountable.
~

I wrote stories, poems, journals, a serious novel;
no one surely not I saw them to praise them
enough to make them public;
I wasted my Guggenheim. My dissertation
on a fierce Frenchwoman was accepted with praises;
I did not type a clean copy, did not submit it,
was not awarded a final degree; I kept
all these papers secret, a private
joke I had no laughter for.
I wrote no reproaches.

I understood my jobs; employers cherished
their fractions of me, praised & used me.
My work was serviceable, subordinate.

I played the parts given me as
written, word-perfect; I never
laid claim to a part, do not know
what would have happened
had I laid a claim.

I was a quick study; I was not a star.

My only excuse lies in what I
observed of the birds; it is faulty;
it shouldn't apply.

Since I was not a success
I must have been a failure.
There is no one to blame
but myself.

AMONG WOMEN

AMONG WOMEN

What women wander?
Not many. All. A few.
Most would, now & then,
& no wonder.
Some, and I'm one,
Wander sitting still.
My small grandmother
Bought from every peddler
Less for the ribbons and lace
Than for their scent
Of sleep where you will,
Walk out when you want, choose
Your bread and your company.

She warned me, "Have nothing to lose."

She looked fragile but had
High blood, runner's ankles,
Could endure, endure.
She loved her rooted garden, her
Grand children, her once
Wild once young man.
Women wander
As best they can.

SUMMER SESTINA

for Rosemary

Her daylilies are afloat on evening
As their petals, lemon- or melon-colored,
Dim and lift in the loosening grip of light
Until their leaves lie like their shadows, there
Where she had hid dry corms of them, in earth
She freed of stones, weeded, and has kept rich.

With dusk, the dense air rises unmixed, rich,
Around our bodies dim with evening;
Creek air pours up the cliff to her tilled earth
And we swim in cool, our thoughts so colored
They can haunt each other, speechless, there
Where bubbles of birdsong burst like mental light,

Among the isles of lilies soaked with light.
We wait for moonrise that may make us rich
With the outsight of insight, spilling there
On her meadow when the moon ends evening
And brings back known shapes, strangely uncolored,
To this earthly garden, this gardened earth.

Deep deep go these dug fertile beds of earth
Where mystery prepares the thrust for light.
Years of leaffall, raked wet and discolored
With winter kitchen scraps, make the mix rich;
The odds against such loam are evening,
Worked on by her intentions buried there.

Why she does it is neither here nor there—
Why would anyone choose to nurture earth,
Kneel to its dayneeds, dream it at evening,

Plan and plant according to soil and light,
Apple, basil, snowpea, each season rich—
What counts isn't that her world is colored

Or that by it our vision is colored,
But that the gardener who gardens there
Has been so gardened by her garden: grown rich,
Grown fruitful, grown to stand upon the earth
In answer to the ordering of light
She lends to us this August evening.

By her teaching there we are changed, colored,
Made ready for evening, reconciled to earth,
Gardened to richness by her spendthrift light.

CURANDERA

In New York cold, few command the waking of spring.
When it is winter it is always winter
For those born New Yorkers who crouch mute over
The stains of hurt they hide to advertise.

But Spanish people in overcoats come,
Personal with their heavy dismay,
To the daughterless lady;
They are clouds that cannot rain here;
She hands them broken white
Candles to put lit like crocus at her windows;
Among them her spirit spins mercurial;
The winds freshen; the sky stoops.
        She thinks about helping, thinks
        Where to shop for the white rose,
        The white bird, in the proper places
        Sets saucers of water on the floor
        Of her Queens house where stereo
        Plays the drums. No dirt floor. No hibiscus.

Often her clothing is white. At times she wears
Spangles as only a woman of virtue can. Her round neck
Is ringed with the white beads of the Merciful
And the red and blue beads of Helper Barbara;
Gold links ring her waist to honor Poverty Champion
Who protects the Seven Great Potentials and us from them.
There are eleven Helpers; she can undertake
Eleven dances to introduce Help to those
Who are clean in the way a tree is clean
During the night of a dancing, inside the Florida
Water ring sprinkled on the floor.

A dancing is a trance she takes.
Sweating cleanses.
If visited so as to become her holy Familiar
She stamps as she turns & smokes his favorite cigar;
Rhythms flow from her high welcoming hand down off as He
Laughs in her throat to clear it for his voice:

> "The mourning dove has black feet because the pink & green
> blessing of daybreak on it must be supported.
> In the box of candles keep always more than seven on a shelf
> higher than shoulder level. Abundance. Respect.
> Never cut across the feathers of the throat.
> If there is in this house broken glass it must be removed.
> If there is in this house a mirror even in a bag it must
> be covered with a white cloth.
> Do not beat on the gates; knock, and be ready."

The dismayed comes out of his overcoat jigging & the moving
Opening of doing keeps going changing
Climate into younger weather in
To the break of day. Relief.

FROM THE FOUNTAIN
AT VAUCLUSE

I

This light is water. In emerald ascent
Pooled at the cliff it has chiseled, it has brought
To light its clear, unsounded affluent.
To its star-planet I am astronaut
Come home. Crowds come with me, intent
On holiday at the Fountain of Vaucluse.
Its vulnerable air brings us up short.

A girl dips her foot in, holding her shoes.
A boy throws stones so splashes distort
The pool; most males do, as if they confuse
Marking with marring; as if, innocent,
Inept at awe, they smash what they can't use
Or ignore, here where joy's intelligent
In the still light bodied by greening blues.

2

My heart steadies here, sensing something taught:
I take this pool holding opening as
The font and vulva of the planet, brought
From depth to light by the soft force it has
And from view to vision by the path it wrought,
Unknown, central, central, earth-old, blue, blue.
They nod to see it, women on the grass:
Some cross the crown of sunlit stone it wells up through
To watch how limpidly it lets light pass
Transparent to itself. Girls stare who,
Woman-trained not to catch but to be caught,
Are not able to shout, throw, sprawl askew.
Here, their malfunction works in them like thought
Transcending the loss of all they do not do.

3

Or so it seems, as girls without parade
Bend to the shoreline, cup their hands, and drink.
Two old women hand themselves down and wade.
Some girls with brothers throw stones; most shrink
As the waters break. They may be afraid
Of breaking anything: *and that is right*
Though praise for it negates what are, we think,
The claims of power. As woman, I take fright
At power in brute strength (here at the blue brink
Of star-borne paradise) which breeds the fight
I shirk but know my people can't evade
While the good, self-bound in either covert spite
Or child-like impotence, watch their good fade.
Landscape be my lens. Rectify my sight.

4

Cockerel, brash, these July boys & men
Cannot love what they have never seen
Or see what pecking greed keeps hid from them,
Trained not to listen for what their lives mean
But to beat. By that blinding stratagem
All lose. Women and men confuse success
With loud failure to work and work serene.
Boys we raise to thrive under cockpit stress,
Faced here with peaceful force, must intervene.

A child trammelled in heeled shoes and ironed dress
Smiles for the blue pool, climbs close to it; then
Her hand if timid touches its face. Yes
I hate her heels and pleats. But praise is sudden
In me for her easy move of tenderness.

5

Another male; three stones; but though I wince
I see what their opposite costs my sons.
They pay high for their gentle difference
From the mindless strength of competition;
Yet even now I am not convinced
That I was wrong (now that they rightly see
Weakness as tyranny, and have begun
To search themselves for true strength, desperately)
To hate unimagining ambition
Which says, "I'll be more," not, "Here's what I'll be."
A worse mistake I have regretted since:
My daughter was not taught priority
For her own work.
                    Could I wash out those prints,
How, how could I now teach them differently?

6

Some women can see only males, and some
See only themselves, as if they too were male.
Both own the bitter equilibrium,
The base, hurt power of slaves. They are the frail
Employers of pity; they are dumb,
Cute, weak at will.
                    My daughter did not learn
Those tricks. She neither flirts nor wails.
Generous & gentle, can she stand firm
Having found her own ground, or will she fail
(I've failed) to use her time and too late turn
To lay her claim? Can her young wisdom
Keep loving-kindness and yet rise to spurn
Unsuitable self-sacrifice?
                    Now come
Two sisters to the pool where water burns.

7

The air above the sun-flamed pool is air
Changing into freshness. The two girls face
The subtle water. One sighs. Both stare
As if the split of mind from will were effaced
At last, by the freshening. They, laughing there,
Are the generation of the world. I see
Women may model a fresh human grace
That is not weak but deep for those set free
Of win & lose, and—present like this place—
Come from depth to breadth by pressing steadily.

A tall old woman whispers, de bon aire,
"Paradisa esta si." Is? Was? Not to me?
I'm confused. Her words startle everywhere.
Daughter, your paradisa is not; may be.

REPLAY, DOUBLED

This light is water in emerald ascent,
Old, holy; this water is where it lies
The font and vulva of the planet, brought
To light to open vision where the wise
Bend to the shoreline, cup their hands, and drink.
Though insight takes girls by sacring surprise
Their hands, if timid, touch its cold face
And know they are the sacred in disguise.
And even now I am not convinced
We would be wrong to worship who we are
As we come to the pool where water burns
Above a course that stone miles could not bar.
Grown from depth to breadth by pressing steadily,
We may stand human on our mother star.

A girl dips her foot in, holding her shoes,
Where all our history has come with praise.
Here her malfunction works in her like thought:
She can bear to be open and amazed
As the waters break. She may be afraid
Of the self-healed stillness that the pool displays,
Its face a peaceful force that intervenes
To soften stone; but it has turned her gaze
From weakness as tyranny, and begun
To model her. She's doffed her steep glass shoes
And the base, hurt power of slaves. She is frail.
She may go home glass-shod and deny this news
Of how to model a fresh human grace.
But she has been here. It is hers to choose.

GHOST WRITER

Irene on my tiny list of answers to despair
I star your name

But now I come to complain.
Lately, you only ghostwrite.
Able, serviceable, conscript
Papers on liverfluke or cattlebone,
Speeches on green research phrased
For a larynx not your own,
Replace in your portfolio the work
I think you were born to,
The personal words.
You have stopped writing those shapes
That leave calm people
                dizzy with listening to
                your truthful speakers
                say their human tunes.

Sensual, intellectual, acute to differentiate:
Sweet realist, you have always ghostwritten
What you can of what you cannot tolerate.
Strange to what sounds stupid
                you light-wristed
Transmute as you catch them
Our banal verbal moves into
                dazzles of juggled idea;
I am a bore but you are not bored; you
Fox me into surprises, for

You ghostwrite your friends too:
As you imagine how we act toward who we are
You better us;

You hear us
          and, entirely pleasant
          in earrings and a silk disguise,
          you glance at the glass you hold,
          you think, fast, speak,
              smile,
          swallow your drink,
And we see what you see we mean.
Then for the pleasures you give us
          you thank us
So discreetly we accept your thanks.

Grace, as it dilates, effaces.
Is this how you become yourself?

You do become yourself.
Even your shy ankles are articulate of it;
Your hair no matter who cuts it is
Crisp as tulips and suits you; your
Voice, when you speak in it, is
Unmistakable, a rationale for words.
             I catch
As it vanishes that chaste voice,
Behind the words, in years of pageants
You wrote for the children for holidays
—lost once played: daylilies, champagne, ephemera:
       Bastille Day birthday high jinks,
       a mime for a dancing giant,
       Noah's arksong, solstice jokes,
       now lost,
Matches written to be lit and lost—
~

You interrupt in your delicate French,
Its irony delicate, "Je regrette . . ."

Yes I regret your lost writing, the woodland
Dry its streams redirected the stories
Left random, left unsaved,
Your sightseeing left unrecorded, lost,
Your language lent.
Yes yet
        no, I take back my complaint.

              I praise your Maygames
              your short always festivals
              their blaze-and-black fireworks,
              the confident gesture of them
              their formidable innocence.
The genius you modulate into helpful use thrives
              despite you,
              as the haunt of your lost lines
              improves your children into celebrants,
                    your friends into imagined action,
                    me into asking
If perhaps a woman
So rich is so free
She can
Sun-brilliant, sun-unseen,
Afford to keep
Herself like a secret, Irene,
And the secret, meekness
              unspeakable
              sanctity

OVERHEARD

1 LOGAN AIRPORT, BOSTON

"Kissed me hello & all that shit; I
Said to him are you
Seeing my sister?
Yes he said.
And she'd swore up and down
It was no such thing,
The picture of her was
      just a place
      looked
      like his backyard.
I got upset.
Seems like most people got to lie to me
Most of the time.
Don't want to break somebody's arm or head or that,
But I sure have got some news to break to her."

2 STUDENT UNION CAFETERIA

"That's not true, 'It don't alleviate nothing.'
What it alleviates
is me bustin my ass, for who
for my father
that's who, not even my mother
          that's another story,
for my father.
So since I got to bust my ass anyhow
I'd just as well move in with Mike
and let my
father
buy himself his own beer."

3 HIGH FALLS MARKET

"Nice little town it was;
Big city grew right on up out to
next door.
Ruined it. Ruined it.
From us to them
We still got 10–15 miles, rural
All rural.
Farmers swear it's going to last.
It won't last."

4 SENIOR CITIZENS' CENTER, QUEENS, N.Y.

"They think it's better for kids to be brought up rich
they should ask my mother. Ask me. My father
big business man cigar and all, worked late worked
nights worked weekends, his big deals,
he didn't even know I was alive.
My mother used to dress me up for him, he never looked,
till I was 18 and wanted to get a job.
He had a fit. His
daughter had
a job, he said, to get a husband,
a Jewish boy, with a rich father business-
man like him and a good job.
So I went and I got married to the poorest
Jewish boy I could find, brilliant,
no job, no head for business,
and poor is no good either.
He was just like my father, he
didn't know I was alive.
With him it wasn't business it was socialism."

THE DIFFÉRANCE:
CHATOU-CROISSY

It was hard, but she was doing it,
Raising him well, the boy
Fathered on her by her mother's lover—
Buying his shoes in name-brand stores
Where fitting took time, keeping his teeth good.
Her skills were domestic, the knife
In her small hands all edge as it flashed
Rabbit flesh, parsley, leeks,
Into sizes she wanted.
When she could, she married a steady boy
Who'd never thought to get so fine a woman,
Who got on with her son,
Who even loved the boy though ashamed of him.

"Yes," she said, "he's of course the boss.
Whatever he says to do
I do, he loves to see me do it,
I never say a word. But now you're married,
I can tell you. Listen, let him be the boss,
Call him boss, all day,
Even in bed, do it his way,
Why not, ça ne coûte rien, and
He's got to sleep sometime:
That's your chance. Every night I wait till he snores,
Then I just lean my elbow into him until
He has to turn, a minute later I just lean
Again, he turns, you see? It's not for nothing
He's got pits of shadows all around his eyes,
The punk. You'll see, you can call him boss,
Boss all day, he'll eat it up,
Late at night, he never knows, you laugh."

LIVE MODEL

Who wouldn't rather paint than pose—
Modeling, you're an itch the artist
Doesn't want to scratch, at least
Not directly, and not yet.
You think, "At last, a man who knows
How bodies are metaphors!" (You're wrong.)

First time I posed for him he made
A gilded throne to sit me on
Crowned open-armed in a blue halfgown.
I sat his way, which was not one of mine
But stiff & breakable as glass,
Palestill, as if
With a rosetree up my spine.
We had to be speechless too,
Gut tight in a sacring thermal
Hush of love & art;
Even songs & poems
Were too mundane for me to quote
To ease our grand feelings
So I sat mute, as if
With a rosetree down my throat.

Now I breathe deep, I sit slack,
I've thrown the glass out, spit,
Evacuated bushels of roses.

I've got my old quick walk
& my big dirty voice back.

Why do I still sometimes sit
On what is unmistakably like a throne?
Why not. Bodies are metaphors,
And this one's my own.

HALF-LIFE:
COPIES TO ALL CONCERNED

Gentlemen: how are you? Here things go well.
I write you after these many years to ask
If you have any news of all I lost
That I'd forwarded to you, insured, I'd thought,
First Class, on urgent demand, with a good
Guarantee (though that would be expired now).

What I miss is not you (as you do, now?)
But the girl I gave you. Did she do well,
That stern young person planning to be good,
Sure of her dress, her footing, her right to ask?
Lovers have half-life in each other's thought
Long after; is the mark she made quite lost?

Have you traces of her? That she got lost
I'd never guessed; but from what I hear now,
You never quite received her, though we thought
She knew more than the directions well
And would get by, skilled in what not to ask.
Were her efforts at lipstick any good?

Did she learn to tell bad eagerness from good?
If you do remember her, then she's not lost;
I've forgotten her so long, I must ask
(I didn't love her then as I might now)
What, for a while, told you you knew her well,
What live cry for her survives in your thought,

Who she was for you, what she meant, feared, thought.
She had trunks, jammed with what her love judged good;
Are they still somewhere, tagged & indexed well,

Or are they like my pictures of her lost?
I've saved what she left—stale or fragile now—
Latin books, laughs, wine, lists of what to ask.

Should you have questions, do feel free to ask,
Given the always present tense of thought.
Though I know no time is as bad as now,
Recall her you—I could!—let him make good
The tale of that naked pure young fool, lost
Before I got a chance to know her well.

I should say, as well: beyond what I ask
Lies the you you lost, alive; in my thought
Still planning to be good. Redeem him now.

Now ask your thought for this lost good. Farewell.

UNABASHED

Unabashed
as some landscapes are
(a lakeshape, say,
lying and lifting
under a cupping sky)
          so angels are,
entire with each other,
their wonderful bodies
obedient, their strengths
interchanging—
          or so
we imagine them
hoping
by saying these things of them
to invent human love.

AS IS

Objects new to this place, I receive you.
It was I who sent for each of you.
The house of my mother is empty.
I have emptied it of all her things.
The house of my mother is sold with
All its trees and their usual tall music.
I have sold it to the stranger,
The architect with three young children.

Things of the house of my mother,
You are many. My house is
Poor compared to yours and hers.
My poor house welcomes you.
Come to rest here. Be at home. Please
Do not be frantic do not
Fly whistling up out of your places.
You, floor- and wall-coverings, be
Faithful in flatness; lie still;
Try. By light or by dark
There is no going back.
You, crystal bowls, electrical appliances,
Velvet chair and walnut chair,
You know your uses; I wish you well.
My mother instructed me in your behalf.
I have made room for you. Most of you
Knew me as a child; you can tell
We need not be afraid of each other.

And you, old hopes of the house of my mother,
Farewell.

NURSING: MOTHER

I

Tranquillized, she speaks or does not speak;
Immobilized, she goes to & fro invisibly.
The names of my children she recalls
Like a declension; my ex-husband is,
She thinks, the verb of a bad dream she had,
Irregular. When she listens,
What does she hear?
Kept in so long after school, it is her wits
That she, old traveller, sends wandering.
                    What joke
Will make her laugh? Doctor
Is she in pain? To her the nurse
Talks loud & slow as to a foreigner;
To whom have age and injury made
This most local woman alien?

Patient, she lies like a paradigm
Elaborate on her fenced high bed because
Her hip-bone snapped. Her doctor
Indicates his neat repair. I flinch
Before her sacredness.

From between those thighs
(Splashed in those days iridescent
With brighter-than-blood mercurochrome)
I thrust into sight thirsting for air
(So it must have been; so my children came;
So we commit by embodying it, woman to woman,
Our power: to set life free.
She set me free).
~

Long closed against me, now her flesh
Is a text I guess to read: Is
She in pain? My own flesh aches dumb
For a mummer's gift of touch
We might use to speak ourselves
Against this last fitful light
To mime the thirst we have.

2

To visit her I go among the graduates
Of ordinary discourse, where wryly
They command them who keep them.
Where they live is hot, rank, preserved,
Lion country.

In state among them Mother
Has her Lying-In as
Infant Empress whose otherness
Confuses the lions
And instructs them tame.

Where I dream she still walks domestic
In a peacock dress, bead-embroidered,
Aloof among my garden's raucous goats.
I dream her as blessing, with birds as gifts;
I dream her as the Tower's Priestess of cruel
Removal and Return, stepping in & out
At her will of her warm shadow, me.
I dream her serene, regent in her own
Diamonded mystery.
~

If I am hers she does not feel it.
The Empress Infant has no child.
She watches their antics as if her look
Kept the subject lions staked and tethered
Where they stalk. But suddenly,
"To see you," she says, "brightens me."

3

Here or dream, she is not at home. She
Can only come home to a boxroom brownstone
For breakfast on fried oysters & talk of the news
Of ships' arrivals in the Sunday *Tribune*
Between a man and woman who love her;
And even the walls of her homing are
Dust these forty years.

What she has kept of who she is
Is what the part calls for: a
Winsome dominance, speaking up
With a half-lost sense of audience; do
They tire of her she sleeps; do they smile
She is glad of it; what is she practicing?
Here on the flat of her bed the size
Of a flat box already ready in a factory.

Empress and Infant fear the toppling of the Tower.
She wishes the visitor were her mother, but
Trying it, saying, "Mom! How's Pop?"
Quickly adds, "Never mind. Never mind."
~

Today she said, "In the sun
Your hair has many colors,"
Quickly adding, "With these glasses
You got me, of course, I'm nearly blind."

LATE

for Marie Candee Birmingham, my mother

1

Dark on a bright day, fear of you is two-poled,
Longing its opposite. Who were we?
What for? dreaming, I haunt you unconsoled.

Rewarded as I force thought outward, I see
A warbler, a Myrtle, marked by coin-gold—
I feel lucky, as if I'd passed a test,
And try my luck, to face the misery
Of loss on loss, find us, and give us rest.
Once we birdwatched, eyeing shrub & tree
For the luck beyond words that was our quest;
Your rings flashing, you showed me day-holed
Owls, marsh blackbirds on red wings, the crest
Kingfishers bear. Mother, dreams are too cold
To eye the dark woodland of your bequest.

2

To eye the dark woodland of your bequest
I wear the fire of diamond on my hand,
Flawed extravagance of your first love expressed
In a many-faceted engagement band.
Recklessly cut with the blaze I invest
In my dazzling flaws, careless of weight,
The fiery cast of mind that I love planned
To sacrifice carat-points for this bright state.
It is yours still, and I go talismanned
By you to find you, though I'm lost & late.
You left this for me; ringed I go dressed
To mother us, mother, to isolate
And name the flight of what, mouth to rich breast,
We meant while we were together to create.

3

We meant while we were together to create
A larger permanence, as lovers do,
Of perfecting selves: I would imitate
By my perfections, yours; I would love you
As you me, each to the other a gate
Opening on intimate gardens and
Amiable there. Mother you were new
At it but when you looped us in the bands
Of clover hope to be each other's due,
The hope at least lasted; here I still stand
Full of the verb you had to predicate.
Though you as subject now are contraband
Half hidden, half disguised to intimidate,
I recognize your diamond on my hand.

4

I recognize the diamond on my hand
As the imagined world where we were whole.
Now among boxed bones, pine roots, & Queens sand,
You have changed places with this bit of coal,
Dark to light, light to dark. To understand
The dark your child never was afraid of
I go lightless sightless birdless mole
In the dark which is half what words are made of;
I enter the dark poems memories control,
Their dark love efficient under day love.
Down I go down through the oldest unscanned
Scapes of mind to skim the dim parade
Of images long neglected lost or banned,
To root for the you I have not betrayed.

5

To root for the you I have not betrayed
I hunt the ovenbird we never found—
Or guessed we'd found when something leafbrown strayed
Under the trees where soft leaves lay year round.
When you'd said, "Hush," and we'd obeyed (obeyed
Lifelong too long) "Tea/cher!" we heard; the shy
Bird spoke itself, "Tea/cher!" from the dim ground
The call came plain enough to recognize
And we went out following the sound.
It went before us in the dusk; its cries
Go before me now, swerve & dip in shade
Woman daughter bird teacher teach me. Skies
Boughs brush tufts; blind I have lost where we played
All trust in love, to the dark of your disguise.

6

Trust in love lost to the dark of your disguise,
I forget if I loved you; I forget
If, when I failed, you requisitioned lies;
Did we make believe we saw the bird, and set
On my lifelong list what my long life denies:
That we found what we wanted side by side?

But I did see you bird I see you yet
Your live glance glinting from leafdust; you hide
Calling, colorless, your brief alphabet
Sharp. Wait, wait for me. Flash past, dusty bride,
Stand safe, rosefooted, before my finite eyes.
Sing, undeafen me. Bird be identified.
Speak yourself. I dread love that mystifies.
Say we wanted what we found side by side.

7

I say I wanted what I found at your side.
("Is that your mother?" yes. "But she's a tea/
cher." yes. I see that.) Reading, sunned, outside,
I see your lit hand on the page, spirea
Shaking light on us; from your ring I see slide
A sun, showering its planets across skies
Of words making, as you read or I or we,
A cosmos, ours. Its permanence still defies
The dark, in sparkles on this page; fiery,
It makes its statement clear: light multiplies.
No matter on whose flawed hand what jewel rides
Or who quickens to what bird with jeweled eyes,
The light of the planet is amplified.
Bird your life is diamond and amplifies.

REPLAY

The luck beyond birds that was our quest
I find in you. Although I'm lost & late
Our hope at least lasted; here I still stand
In your dark love, efficient under day love;
It goes before me in the dark, its cries
Sharp. Wait, wait for me. Flash past, dusty bride,
Make your statement clear: light multiplies.

HOMMAGES

HOMMAGES À CHARLES PERRAULT

Once there was a king the old man writing
his heart out wrote who had a daughter
and whose dearest wife was dead.
Now this princess ("not yet fifteen") was
beautiful comme le jour
et le petit jour as the day
as the dawn of day is beautiful.

Charles ageing elegant and grand
absolute owner of several styles
shut over his own verse book
declined many desirable invitations
rose early, mornings, and went walking among new
statues down the hazegreen vistas spry with birds
court cats and children playing in the royal
pleasure gardens of the Tuileries.
Statues children creatures presences
moved around him softly made him move
around and down around the riverhaze spring vistas
turning in a hushing lilt of echoes
soundless over the ordered grounds
among shy welcome whisperings and laughing cries.

They saw him home, came in, and stayed
liminal, watching among the hours of the afternoon,
until he sat and wrote to net
in his steady tall fine script
shimmering young girls who came alive, in flower-
embroidered gowns, jewel-crowned, attended,
or in loose silks, gone flower-gathering.
~

The old man dredged. The murexed fables
fish-flashed up, a catch that had enchanted once
an upon-a-time petit Charlot
when his nurse or rarely mother
scared and satisfied him so.

He wrote, to satisfy his presences,
for every era rank and age of man
        himself especially
        bonhomme bon père bon mari
        bon bourgeois de Paris
(except for sanitary wives whose
germless infants sicken easily,
except for those whose sanitary
lives lack love enough to be afraid
who harbor what they must deny
gnomes witches ogres wicked
second marriages).

Lucid, addressed by secrets and slight presences,
hiding them with light, he addressed himself to these . . .
Red-wristed girls in from Nancy and St-Lô
alone, indoors, in the evening with only
another woman's brats to comfort and take
comfort from, poor driven maids, could climb
to their cold attics glowing, having
spelled out how high poor driven maids may go
telling aloud the bedtime tales of the Perrault.

Young women of the great families, even
those who practiced intelligence, became

the picture of mothering, his "Histoires
ou contes" in hand, awaiting the occasional
ceremony of the children's visit.
Noble ears heard their own diamond-cut
-diamond world in that perfectly
acceptable noble prose   hearing, really,
tunes neglected hearts like theirs
might dance a measure of, crying on dear wishes,
imaginary innocence, undistracted limbs,
and a sleep reflecting petals
fast among the slowly opening
roses of forever-after love.

He intended, too, the smiles over small heads at his wit, that
famous in its day had all Paris laugh as Perrault saw fit;
he intended to have the smilers' sleeping bravest longings
stirring to be spoken of, unsmiling, under it.
"What's your cause, old man?"
      "Myself. And I have pled it well."
Innocent of causes, his fancies freed him too;
a costly freedom, even in an age of skilled extravagance
a brilliant and abandoned buy. The discipline of years
held good: only a third of his heroes are hideous
: splayed, humped Ricky, and the Beast, and how
splendor of person came upon them
being loved by heroines not yet fifteen

(and what Bluebeard, unloved, became)

how all advisors but the ugly lover fail
(what had Bluebeard been, obeyed?)
~

and how royal love-matches reward
love that can take pity and keep faith.

But children, listening
hear with children's passionate hearing
the sounds of the stories and wait to take
the moment when the known voice makes
a shape and it's the magic word
                    is it the stained
found key to Bluebeard's nest, or the leggy
wolf's big appetite, or the ass who crapped out
little piles of gold in coins,
is it all the lovely girls "not yet fifteen"?

It is death and gaming, quick-come sighs of joy,
now unmerited, now earned by pluck propriety or love;
extempore, eternal, terrible, and all quite true.

Confirming children's knowledge of the world,
he yet allows them hope.
He gives them, see, quiet and clearly
surrounded by sun in a radiance of air
among small grasses pied with flowers
a few flower stalks in her hands
the girl who is glory and gold
simply, where she stands.
                    He also gives
infinite permissions to be a child
and all the persons children are;
even the well-known secret witch must leave
her cave of shadows and come out

wearing a name it's safe to say aloud
to meet the well-known secret powerful
godmother gifted and gifting with her wand.
It is ourselves we make as he makes us believe.

Nights of nightmares ripen into dreams; splintery
facts round out into shapes of stories for
children moving toward their truth, advancing
constant and glorious on the rich real world
as they courageous under the covers keep
growing up, sleep by troubled sleep.

GRAND MOTHER TO MIRANDA

for Muriel Rukeyser, who says,
"I'd rather be live Muriel than dead Ariel."

As grace to wit is courage to Muriel;
Her song says though its voices are various,
"There is no truth that is not usable."

The drawn line, the equation, the syllable
Each tells her truths equally curious;
As grace to wit is wisdom to Muriel.

In strike or stroke, tragic or comical,
Her sight unblinds us to what's serious:
There is no dream that is not usable.

Model & mother, her mind makes visible
The great world she claims as home for us;
As grace to wit is justice to Muriel.

From *Flight* to *Gates* her hope grows more radical;
It shows us search is never impious
And there is no growth that is not usable.

Intimate of Caliban as of Ariel
Her voice improves the gentle & the furious;
As grace to wit is woman to Muriel:
There is no truth that is not usable.

OF CERTAIN STUDENTS

Once, teachers were giants of the numinous
—Plato, Plotinus, Porphyry, Iamblichus—
Whose sandaled academies trod holily on air;
I praise them but (in class) am not envious.
Ritual can't spin up out of the likes of us;
We're safe.
   Yet we, not even friends, do exchange
Fierce energies. Playing at change,
We do change. Sometimes, you gesture and
From off your hands blades of light flash.

Sometimes in your absences
I turn you into lists of things
To do, and do them.

Often in your presences
I make lists, in the thinlooped snares
That language casts, of things I ought to say
(And you could sing them)
Great things—and some days your tongues
Are so quick they spring them.

FOR JOHN KEATS

on the sense of his biography

Cold,
John Keats coughs and spits blood.
And in the space
between the meaning and the dream, still does.
It spoke. He heard it, the bright arterial word.
Dying, he tried to exchange himself for verbal
closure of that space. Trying, having sealed
his present for us, he died.

Though many brutal English winters since
have struck the wet heath cold through
the lowest layers of its stone
& as many May weeks sunsteamed it into
a carpet thick with soft
explosions of short flowers,
to praise Keats' presence now helps me.

When he said he wanted to write successfully
Keats meant commercially, planned to arrange
a marriage of his gift with Byronic
cash & fame,
planned to dazzle his girl some day with diamonds
replacing amethysts. Through that promising
dream (trying for audience, shaping his skills)
the spring sun shone when friends and the woman
presented him with promises.
He became the clement season he needed,
plenteous in language
as in primrose the garden was, he breathing
between the cut grass and the plum
tree as if his were the coming

unbudding of summer, for a while.
Words rushed for him toward ripening
and, like full summer in the plums,
flushed in the shaping crystal of his glass;
their long light became the Keats we summer in.
The answer to winter is such saved time.
It is how he keeps us warm.

He had further to go, though; soon
the spot flew vivid from his throat
onto the linen pillowcover
and, bowered in by cotton fields of flowered lawn,
he began the life of what it is to die.
With riches, diamonds, and his darling girl
                a bankrupt fantasy,
close to the comfort of his narrowing bed,
he brided his burden, married
his person to his voice. Mouth on mouth
lost in each other they enclosed
the soundless now of his necessity,
making love present gratuitously
                as the pulse & tune, in what he wrote, of
                what he did not write: his history,
until one day
the birds fell silent for
the singing of the tree.

Though nothing lives that does not die,
nothing dies that does not live.
The price of death is life.
The doctor in him died to find that out;

the lover in him died
           to shine for us
on the leafy life we bear to our exchange with death.

Full of blood or words his mouth
lifted up the shape of the present tense.
That present is the secret poets dare not keep
or tell. It makes them mind. It makes them speak.
Some of them stuff the script of their saying
behind the books on a shelf or under
the other papers in the drawer, startled
if caught making audible the
name tuned beyond union or disunion,
ashamed to have let the tenor of the now
escape upon the loud wind script can go cold in.

As leaf and branch speak flight and water
Keats both keeps and speaks the secret,
quieting that fear
for the rest of us. When
he happened to his writing,
his future disappeared.

I sit outside his Hampstead house & estimate
the age of the mulberry tree.
They say it was old in his time.
It looks young to me.

OUR LADY

for Marilyn Hacker

The thing about you, Mary, thank you,
is that you are grounded where we are
when we are trying to do well;
your truth is not conciliar
but ours and actual.
You are not Bona Dea but Bona
certainly, bona femina,
mulier, woman, wanted, insulted,
a woman like us, like me
though enshrined in seacliffs,
high places, caves, deep cathedrals,
and wherever fresh water springs or falls.
You are known
for nothing
       but that you had free will
       and that once gravida
you proved that birth, perceiving
a new perceiving point, renews;
you proved
women may suffer but do not die
of solitude work love or loss.
When all you had was what you lent,
you sang, you sang.
I tell the strong poet this & she smiles,
your smile (joy undifferentiated
in the speed of assent)

FOR A SEASON

We saw we had few words to exchange when two by two
By two over our heads birds like omens flew
Making space between us dangerous.

      Glances can be truthful; this I learned
      When with your sharp breath the time turned
      Very sharp and felicitous.

And truth is unknowable. Who knows
How far to where the loving goes
When its action makes free of us?

      Generously we lay together
      Under the Irish weather.
      It was summer due to us.

ON THE COUNTRY SLEEP
OF SUSANNE K LANGER

Though she lives there as the wood's
human creature, "carrying water,"
though in her sound shoes she is native to it,
the land even the boundary river
      even when she sleeps
centers about her;
        centered it tenders
its myriad finalities
sunning them
in her energy of shaped ideas.

Focus of the forest focus
of the continent's intelligence
minded in the lucent
patience of her appetite
Susanne K Langer doctor
thankless for wisdom's sake
entertains giant
ghosts, ours & her own; introduces
ideas to each other, reconciles
caves & skyscrapers of selves,
to become a familiar
of where the spirit lives
until even her sleep
is contemplative.

As beginning & end of that act she informs
her forest house.
To watch her in the high wood the night
is willing to be dark.
Beside her raised bed are pencils, yellow,

one in a mottled notebook keeping
her place. Between earth
and elsewhere,
wisewoman, sleeping,
she keeps her place.

Tabled on upstate clifftop
bedrock New York Susanne is lifted up

and though about her the moonlight were
just moonlight,

she lies generic inside
the steep hush of the grove,
earthwoman, offered as
a symptom of our health through
treecrowns & expanding atmosphere to
the skies.

In so focal a biography such sleep
recalls the cast of sacrifice.

LULLABY

Sleep now, hush my
fragile beast,
fed new child, sleep.
Look at you, soft,
life locked to you
safe in your fist;
no light enters yet
like flowers you retain
all the light there is
blotted up like a stain.
Even at dusk you lie,
though this room looks east,
luminous in it; the shadows
stoop so you are centered
as you leach from the air
the last of the light
to show you as holy
as you are fair.
Sleep now. There there.
Good night.

ANTENNAE

Though I like to recline or lie
like the horizon in contact, Dame Kind,
flat out for you as I will more
closely one day be,
I get up when you turn to the light
and stand what I call tall.
Small
my feet flat to their task
at least one always touching you,
my head stuck out further
than my feet by what
I call an important distance,
an oracular one (these differences
of distance between head & feet
being what there is of me),

I look around at us your short
antennae, little bristles, erect if
crookedly so, mobile—
and I admire our stance.
We are brave our heads
sticking out kangarooed
in your generous pocket;
I admire our power to imagine you,
our plots to lighten your burden & lift
ourselves to your beyondness, outside
the nourishment of air.

I admire the tenuous delight feet
take toward you in flatness,
admire what of your voice we have

that keeps speaking you, setting
waves of complicating sound surging
with daring over your continents,
while my bones not unlike your trees
hold my significant if not
readily defensible length
upright & interested,
for part of each day,
for decades of years.

A THIRD THANK-YOU LETTER
for the gift of the Vert-Galant

The Seine and the sky refract each other's rain.

Unrefracting, I
lost June looking for you.

Every river needs an island
to underline its wetness with
that surge of green plume
every island needs.

And here, among the green where
the curve of the river ramparts retains
the river in stone, and the curves in pencil
retain the pulse of these words,
you are.

It is after all late spring; I write,
"You are here, after all."
For the rest of the morning
I do not need to remember
anything; for the rest of the day
there is the morning to remember;
I think we remember it together.

The blunt barge nose slowly shows
the middle bridge arch has been chosen, and
glides under; behind
the long flat of it, the person with
bright mind in the less bright white
wheelhouse looks down over coal-
heaps at Vert-Galant, glances with

your brightness,
waves and grins
above the integrating water.

In the July mist I welcome you.

You offer me the river, grey
as the sky but glaucous like Homer and
olive leaves or like puddles of oil paint
cupping dark green & pulsing silver
in every direction.

Babbling, I've missed you.
In St-Séverin I did not see the pillar I
talked about though it leapt up like
you for us, living, the line emerging
from the stone in three dimensions yet
linear therefore envisioned and springing
clear as mind from living brain.
I am in fact usually
much too busy to look for you.
No wonder I catch cold. The casual
river does better, always watching the sky.

Opposite, along the outer thigh of the given river,
some trees are missing from the row, plane trees
gone to lighten traffic where the toy
cars speed toward Notre Dame (you
are, in them, less reflected than you are,
my brightness, by the river
though their metal winks for you boldly). Today
~

the river is what you have given me,
and the locust the willows the chestnut
of the small in-position park, emerging head-down
from the river's undulant pelvic floor,
lying along the modular inner thighs of the river
new green to encourage the signals
of new lovers, games of new children, new
farewells of old voyagers.
            Because I have been here
watching and in place for one hour
you have come flooding back to me
bearing ransom. Awash with that limpid
identity, I take you in. All islands are
always being born; each needs
a like inhabitant, interacting, riverborne:
here I am, just down from the palace of justice
greening, crowning, new at the feet of Notre Dame,
assuming your welcome
and welcoming you
gratefully

grown to want
what I have
and to have
what I want
where I want
what I have
to be

DISCOVERY

DISCOVERY

Though I sit here alone I
am smiling and
realize why as I find
that the answer (to my own
old poser of who will be
my magna mater) is clear;
I can even understand
her invisibility
for she, the grand
mother (I've always needed)
    is surely here
      too close to see
      for I am she.
Laughing she explains nothing.

My life is given back to me.

For we survived seedtime
(some seeds pop their pods and jump away;
some eased out of clumps by gold birds
float off, alight, and again drift;
some, deer after drinking drop
near a pleasant stream) we
survived and the winter
was kind to the seed
and now the winter has lifted;
I leave the season of need.

Daughter gone to lover of daughter,
sons to lovers of sons, all
have gone from me readily

with the extended almost soundless leap
of trust in genital clemency.
Left to myself I discover
that what had to spring together
has sprung together and the fields
are beds of blossoming,
the hollow meadows fill
again with blossoming.

Blessing the gardeners I do not doubt
the benefits the blessing yields
as daily less anxiously
I walk out among them
or windsoft beyond them
unheard unheeded
not lost not needed
reaching invisibly
for what is great yet proper to me
and cannot but mother me:
unconsidered liberty.

FIELD OF VISION: A MAP
FOR A MIDDLE-AGED WOMAN

I

      The wind changes; I slept in it
Like a stone awash at the bottom of the stream.
With the sun, the mist and I rise.
        I fall upward to wake outside
        The numbered myths of measure
        Into real time.
        I fall awake beyond
        The distancing myths of memory
        Blinking to see
        Measurelessly.
Mortal eyes, mine, seeing almost
A hemisphere at a time, here see
It is late summer, a shimmering.

At my foot, flat up to face the sparse
Light of the clifftop orchard, grow
Furred, rounded (feel!) leaves
In the lee of a sitting stone; overhead
Among old boughs a few apples gleam.

I have never seen anything like it.
It is lonely (lone in likeness, singular),
Lovely (that is, like love). Orphan,
I know no other seasons; unlicensed,
I am not a country person; what I see
Is that nothing real happens twice.
Twice, nothing happens. Grasshoppers' angles
Differ; each jump of theirs links known to new.
My childhood Flying Dutchmen are no clue to these.
Memory's to think with, not daydream absently—
It should be like light on leaping, rain on water,

To make the mind run richer, a brilliance
Merging emerging in the shimmering interchange.

Naming the four points of their land, East first,
The old Celts stood still, then spun to name as fifth
The unity of the four, finite yet mobile,
The space of authority, their sacred place.
In our cooler categories we observe
Six locatives looking left, right,
Up, down, fore, aft: Pines, appletrees,
Blue space through branches, a subtle hill,
Earth grassed & flowering, a cliffedge
Treed. Six. Three pairs. And?
   and I
   am here:
   I name a
   center a
   point of view place,
   fluid;
   as two-handed I go
   on the ground among trees
   toward trees, under the sun,
   away from the hill.
This seventh this perceiving
Point may or may not be
Perceived. I feel perceived,
Perhaps as part of my perceiver,
Where I stand sniffing the morning wind
Determined to take my time, to make it clear,
And—maybe—to conceive of memory.

2

It's hard work.
I can't just abandon the treasure and
Rubble of my inner cities that extend
Beyond where memory gone dim
Is a lens in mist
That by distortion lies.
It won't dissolve. It greys the air with twists
Of ghosts: vain accusers, or lovers, or the dead,
Or at best, echoes, unfair to their vivid origins.

I shout attack
Through the spun-glass atmosphere:
Paris I have never walked your rings; what's
A nightingale? Dowth never have I entertained
Your populous earthwork beyond the fish-inscript
Lintel down the dry passage
At the bottom of the well.
I never met anyone
At the top of the stairs on Christopher Street.

Poems, rock stars, I've never caught
Your new acts on the festival circuit of languages
I never patched light-shows for.
Words, tuned to your own meanings, amps off,
Don't parade in a razzma of overtones
Across the acoustic field
Between me and whatever whispers here.
Lover,
Hard haunched, I have never
Worked trapeze with you

(Or you, lion-maned,
Or you, brandy-splashed, or)

If in strong sun I shout and
The false protective lens or mist
Burns off, if I do without them,
Originals revive.
Daughter, sons, born
Out of the pulsing channel of me,
You consented, each to your own acts,
When at the last breathless moment
You turned your face away from mine
And shouldered, springing, into life
Breathing your lonely breathing
That is like love.
I now disenchant
The frozen totems of your names.
I bid the powerful mystery
That shrouds your names and shrouds
Other loved names of great power over me,
Evaporate. My ears,
That have listened for you
As you no longer are,
Want a hush now and the new.

3

Too bad I can't juggle up a rite of departure
With classic control & in traditional costume
But I have no stage directions.
To be quit I must pay off the worst of you

Vulgarly
          or you'll come on tour with me
By mistake or for blackmail. You ghosts,
Reluctant to go, claim me by false shame:
          shame of lies,
Shame of turning my head lazily away,
Shame of wishing debts paid, owed letters mailed,
Silly shame of missed cues, shame of grief
In brutal places I did not change;
The guilt is mine and I dismiss you;
You are ugly and powerful with sorrow

          sorrow sorrow
          child of comparisons

How will I live without the shaming sorrow
I have dwarfed in a body of selfishness?
So far so good, I walk solid
In a daylight field of vision.
Though the woman walking is
Only me I am central among flashing
Differences (leaves like needles, leaves
That touch like fingers, leaves like islands,
The thousand ingenious ways of being green)
I can watch accurately and see
The little less than an eyelid difference
Between seeing in or out, diminish
Among the shimmering.

4

A maple has thrust roots back in among the rock
Half down the cliff I'm on top of (I am not
A city person). Its leaves wall an aerial
Tunnel that opens into a changing frame for
A mist, maybe off sunned water, rising;
Beyond it lie the shapes
Of a woodland, a pasture, someone's
                                    someone else's.
Barkbrown, scuppering in short arcs, bug catcher,
Bird, I am new here: who are you?
No bird is alien when every wing is strange.
In the newness of strangeness what flights
I may contain I can't guess. Without guidebook,
Unrehearsed, where I climb,
Each shape to take the air
Is the only; all are first;
None last.
I can tell the difference.

Apples sweet with old storms,
Old fires of sun, tasty, eaten
In extreme hunger—I exchange
Their old life for mine.
For ripe fruit
Thank the tree;
And I will yet thank me, if
Splotched still with dried time
I can be washed unstiff of history,
If inside the outside of me
Is me.
~

Good-by apples; grow, grow,
Other travellers' guts will welcome
Your fiery sugars
                    not I, not again;
Abandoning the orchard I quit claim
To satisfaction changed, celled, stored
In the tight-skinned shapes of time fulfilled.

Down in the stream I sandscrub off the camouflage
Loonlight, sunspots, troublers of vision,
Moonstains of schedules, the last
Stiff, eclectic freckles, until
I can't contract for anything.

MAUVE

Last night a few beads or half-
moon spots in the grass
prophesied this shining. Reflections wink
on leaf and blade that the wind tips;
the glint of their fresh life is soft.
It is the moment of spring mauve
when certain tulips, ajuga,
and species bleeding-heart offer together,
blued down from frank pink, their
cups spikes and two-centered
flimsy bells. They rise a little
above the new green, and tilt
in the water-sounding air
full of lilac fall.

It could be any year of the last fifty
that I move among them (we never lose
our first lilacs; I stir here
and up absent avenues
layers of that smell drift,
under this smell, magnetic) as if
as once I were ignorant
not of doing
but of knowing
about having to.

ADVICE:
AD HAEREDITATES, I

The water:
      I pour it
      with care
into these seven jars for
you seven,
sacred voyagers
soon to be launched.
      One of you will
one day need it;
I have seen signs
      in your faces; one
      will need it.
Each of you is
I judge able to need it.

I pray this good water
be to your hand in time of want.

I look into your faces o
my God my children!
      (yes, such talk, the least-
      considered catch of the heart,
      makes pagans guess false worship.
      Well, not their fault; they do not
      know there is one difference
      language does not make.)

You suppose, my seven, that you too
are pagan, my lovely children. When
your turn calls, you will
      lose the lift of doubt.
~

You are setting out now.
I may not be here when you
      come back. Two or three
may find me still around
or find me elsewhere,
on the road or in
grandbabies' faces; sooner or later.
however, we meet again.

You have a taste of the water,
      coronal, in the small
      vials you always carry.
In case you need it, in case
you've half forgotten the true
flavor when someone wants to
sell you lots of wetness
and you need something sustaining,
      or in case
dreaming you dream you are no longer
refreshed by thinking of drinking it—
well, my children, in any such
great emergency
      go ahead,
      break the vial open,
drink your drop, you
won't be able to forget the flavor, then.
Being grown up, having
chosen it and tasted it again,
you may ache
for all—yourself too—who are
usually thirsty but

you won't be unsure of it;
no one ever is, or has been in my
time or my mother's either.

For there is never as much water
available to share or store as we'd like,
never. Nor do most of us manage
to give enough time to locating
new springs and keeping
old sorts of jars, vials, bottles
both safe and accessible. I hear
they do it better, in some places
nowadays; they have special processes.
Probably, voyaging, you'll learn
improvements in methods I haven't
dreamed of. That's progress. For instance,
one way my mother didn't know, I learned
on a voyage of my own: Be dry be as dry
with yourself as you can, so as to
absorb what you need in passing
from the ground or right from the air.
It can happen. Though you miss
the shocking joy of taste,
it will do you its good anyway.

Now, I must say that I have not
tried hard enough, left you enough
except for emergencies, even in quantity. That's
not the worst though: I haven't foreseen
every emergency. There too
I did not do as well as I was able.

But you will forgive me,
those of you anyway who never face
emergency I failed to foresee.
　　　The one who does meet it
head-on will not forgive me
　　　　unless
　　　　maybe
　　　　after.
When you separate, try
to remember to say
(at least! to yourself)
some little
ceremonious
good-by;
take leave
of each other
gracefully.
It saves agony later
when you meet again.
The old ceremony,
the effort you gave it, will
stir your memory warmly,
children.

I've often heard,
"The greater the quantity
the less the thirst in & around you,"
therefore these jars—though
I believe those who say
one drop can suffice
for a lifetime, and no lifetime

lacks that drop. Some disagree;
you'll see for yourselves.

What we know for certain
is that this is water
—mine to give you
what I may of it—
that nothing
can spoil.

ADVICE:
AD HAEREDITATES, II

I

What it is to fall
    (down through the high
    terror of a world gone all
    one Midas color, gold, and I
    deaf to every voice but one)
in love, and the joy of that, I recall.

While I praise the incomparable
attitudes, the touching disguises,
the notice desire takes, intimate as sun,
of the beloved as it day by day devises
bars of delicate jealous reasons for
the prison of the univocal,
        I recall
the failures that follow on
being everything to anyone,
& the excuses for failure that collect to rise
like fog before love-stricken eyes
to dim love's simpler cruelties:
    dinners missed, work abandoned,
    friends' addresses lost, and all
    so that one more deaf gamble
    for ecstasy eternal
    might go down—
and I long
to make a joke of my great ignorance
and yours, to say that as a way
of learning other human beings are
alive, such comic ordinary deafness may
be the only way, and harmless, so long
as lovers keep in mind the chance or hope

of hearing universal song.
For hearing may be restored:
in autumn in America where
we are the migrants there are
never nightingales but now, if there were,
I'd be able to hear them.

2

To be able to hear again is to begin to be
among other persons, intimately free.
If you can hear your lover without fear, hear
friends and value that, listen even to blood
relations you trust as couriers, carriers,
you will—entertaining such harmony—
learn it is not bleak it is like music and
imagining music, to be out of love.
It is the next instrument to smile to be
first nowhere
in no heart first,
never deaf (to every voice but one),
first on no list of invitations,
first to the decency of no enterprise.
You will know
should the purser shriek Fire, the sirens
confirm him, the ship burn, everyone
you included would first rather
save someone other than you.
You will like to become
a person nobody would destroy
or die to rescue, to be

useful, yes tuneful, but expendable;
as loss, to be small loss
so that those bereaved of you would care
(as is good for everyone, to care)
might grieve, might cry out once remembering
on waking some small characterizing thing
but no more than might be good for them.

To imagine this music
choose as instrument something small
(finger bells would do)
so most quartets can form
without you; practice singing
in chorus, joyfully, and learn
to listen as you sing.

3

Although I have chosen it or
it has chosen me,
I'm still afraid to claim
I can keep such tunes harmoniously—
afraid that when in the night the ship
cracking & flaming between
two unsustaining darks
is wrecked
I will still long to rush to place
my chosen one safe in the last lifeboat letting
the rest shriek unheard & go down if need be.
That fear is why
random & ambient,

waiting for more
than the budding of wisdom,
waiting for its fruit & fruitful core,
which may surprise me at the core,
I stay ashore.

Though in my many-voiced harbor city
there are no nightingales, I take
pleasure in the signals starlings make,
in the definite lessons
they know in their hollow bones
how to give their successors: "Cats
kill us," & "Squirrels raid our nests,"
they can say with an eternal starling
agreement; they say, "We eat this grain,"
"We can kill other fledglings for food,"
"We bank to turn," consistently.

If I envy them it's for your sake,
to excuse the confusion, children,
of the way these lines break
like boys' voices under my uncertain
unstarling working definition of the human
music. For the wingless human mind
no form of instruction is modular,
& most true words lie, before
they can be cut in stone.
Of course you know all this already, know
your thoughts are secret as your bones,
no matter how well you learn a beloved,
how much you work to be learned, or

how deaf you walk within desired joy;
your skin is a limit all your own.

Thanks to the admitting ear
we learn to hear as we begin to sing
until (shaking our bells) we have grown
to overhear love as it mingles its voices,
each accidental voice (ours too) essential
and original, a signal for alone.

ADVICE:
AD HAEREDITATES, III

I drop in on you; we all encircle
one table again, & I realize
for the old kinds of listening between us
it is at last too late.
Now I don't like to talk to
you my darlings, as darlings,
though I still have all our history to say.
I carry its weight heavy as infant eyelids
and as secret, untransferable.
I carry packs of albums, films, old toys,
first-grade schoolbags, elixirs healthful
or fatal, none false, all out of date.

My baggage belongs to you, yours to lose or store,
mine to get rid of and walk the lighter for;
but I can't just hand it over any more.
I must let it go. Will you find it? you may.
(All mistakes are only temporary anyway.)
Magic is only a language women once
invented for mute men; you are not mute;
so these things of words I could have crooned or droned
when we were wordless prophets of your world
I let drift away as we sit here, adult,
and otherwise articulate.

What matters is not what they are—all common stuff—
but what they assert of their direction; they came
aimed from where you were once to where I was,

& since we are nowhere near there now
they drop into their proper orbit
not lost but declining; they
spiral and will (drawn into gravity
through the silence of mine to the center of your
memory) fall to rendezvous, come home.

A PROPRIETY

Trees are the rich man's
flowers or the giant's
                or the idler's;
they stand compatible in kinds in
the landscape—locust fringing pine—
like slow bouquets
composed by infants to be
enjoyed by the very old,
        wild bouquets assembled in
        selecting seasons of patience
                        endurance
                        eventual
        impatient failure to endure.

Constellations are gatherings
for those older
vaster or idler still or
for children and the landless
        who can have
        no space to imagine as earth
        of their own and garden in—
and so inherit all the sky.

ANTI-ROMANTIC

I explain ontology, mathematics, theophily,
Symbolic & Aristotelean logic, says the tree.

I demonstrate perspective's & proportion's ways.
I elucidate even greyness by my greys & greys & greys.

Gravity's laws, the four dimensions, Sapphic imagery,
Come from contemplating me,
Says the tree.

I rightly exhibit the functions of earth & air:
Look up at & through my branches, leaved budded or bare
Laid lustrous in their degrees against infinity,
& your seeing relates you to all of space, through me.
Here's aesthetics, too. No sight's nearer to perfectly fair.
I am mediate and immediate, says the tree.

I am variable, exquisite, tough,
Even useful; I am subtle; all this is enough.
I don't want to be a temple, says the tree,
But if you don't behave, I will be.

HARDSHIPS OF THE
ORDINARY ASTRONOMER

On summer nights when after much sun
the temperate flesh is ready to lie out
in the meadow & study, all the wide high
air's awash and flickering;
stars crowd in thickets; they brush in,
brush out of sight, swamping
the map in mind.

This winter night when feet & face
long to navigate closely the radial
ambience of stove,
the heavy cold
declaims the stars' courses.
They stand out in the glass and propose
their formations, which advance engraved,
each distance visible, for those with
shelter and strong instruments.
Short of sun, we can't face the cold
long enough to learn
if other suns can warm.

Our sun we glory in. It clothes
& clocks us obedient to what
we can afford to admit of light.
It hides us from the galaxies, and them,
for a while, from our sight;
its dark hides us daily
though apparent dark has passed.
Even if aloft, where we drift
immersed in sunwash,
we do not imagine

under how much human night
our day is cast.

Drawn
—though confused by our longing—
to acclimatize our vision to what
we think are night skies,
we choose coordinates, set up
the tripod, save up for the lens.
We study charts with a pleasure
made modest by knowing
whatever our algebra aims at,
it is ourselves we measure.

Yet it is the personal
that links us body to body
in the gigantic intercourse, fugal
among the spheres. We are in person those
who, though our sun's dark interferes,
are drawn and stare and listen
to catch tremendous vestiges.
Our hands,
where the capacity inheres, record
what we have caught; our eyes,
able to, read what other hands report.

Though we suppose
that personal time comes
close as sleep to silence
while the faithful heart knocks softly in its cage,
and suppose that kept time is louder though

it only ticks or hums
            according to our pleasure,
we know we are children in what we suppose,
having no ear or other acoustical
devices nor any lens or
vehicle that can come
anywhere near there where the principal
brilliance linking the galaxies
incorporates unmediated

            our mortal loud
flutes, bass fiddles, drums.

NATIVE SPEAKER

Half an hour till my first class,
Student Union cafeteria, the *Times,*
a cup of coffee at an orange table
between the artificial & the window light,
good mornings, bad news; editorials
about locusts & primaries tell the time of year
but not what year it is; I forget and
it's another breakfast as I
think of you
a smallest thought but it scalds
like a splash of fresh birdblood, hot hot that
blisters wishes so their dead skin peels
and all my other thoughts are pinker, flushed,
their nerves at surface.
                                        Listen,
you who can't hear anyway,
anyone who thinks of you
speaks another language right away,
an English so edged accurate intricate
it is yours only, only your
own mother tongue.
And how you do go on: you say
words in your language
again in my head, yes that's your
resonance, the intimate
economy of your scorn for falseness
(you a terrible liar for that reason)
oh I can hear warnings
                            warning me but I
remember anyway I curve
into the curve of your voice as if

into kind arms, savage again
& happy as when you held me holding you, I
forget why I left you, the *Times*
shakes a little in my hand, good mornings
shake a little in my throat, daylight
shakes in the sight you taught
of human beauty; it stirs in these faces
of live beings who have true speech,
whose hands have worked to wire them with words
recorded, until their flesh is all first love.

Someone once told me he thought that you
when last heard from talked like me.
I know I used to try to talk like you.
I don't know; maybe I still do.

GARDEN: PAEONIA
"SOUVENIR DE MAXIME CORNU"

The ground wants rain. Crouched here
I know it better than my own name
And doubt it less; if weeding I kneel low,
Very low, or lie flat, what difference—
It is a self-explained stance
For a person pulling weeds. Daughter
And mother, sustaining member,
A joke, a joker, an account,
Another Christ, a trespasser—
Crookedly, with passion, by chance,
The haphazard selves crisscross
As they drift making no distinction
Among the living the dead the lost.
On an ageless planet I plant
A city garden; I try to keep
Phone books numbered and alarm
Clocks punctual; friend, penitent,
Audience, am have been must
Soon and can never be; can't
Since aiming fatally to please
Grasp and am without rest
Absurdly none of these.

Out here all weathers. Indoors, none.
I juggle, jump-turn, jig, to face
As a paradox the clock-wise places
I also with dim despair perceive
As a continuum
        in which everyone
How do we do it does believe.
The extempore dead could I suppose

Describe my location, if asked.
Deaf-mute we living, though we labor
At loving, are as if invisible one
To the other, despite much love.

I ask them, finally. "Mary and William.
Edward? Elizabeth. Joan."
And bend weeding the black ground
Around the plunged roots of a peony tree
Flowered with tongues of silken flame
Named for a woman on the horns of memory.
Peacefully present, the dead make no sound.

Of the most cherished among
The cherished living, I can see
Six playing croquet shaded by boughs
Of May-laden cherry and pear.
I pose no question there.
I claim no right to answers anywhere.
Pleasure lover, I love my worlds that rouse
So many pleasures, being mutable and fair.

Who am I? Who am I, that I should care?

Until in the midst of the green
Growing, this garden that I tend
With touching, out of a forgotten year
You sharp as love come clear.
Contraries flash into focus as
The promising morning draws to an end;
I am a woman, kneeling here.

I am a place in which you appear.
          Once we shared a city we have left.
          I think it back, that slum-jammed
          Dazzling citadel. Clocks crack,
          Admitting history. Stranger, sweet
          Acquaintance, you would rather be
          Disguised as a stopwatch or shotglass
          Or calm certificate of bonded dividends
          But you speak, you say my name,
          And say, "The ground wants rain.
          It will rain soon"; I agree
And suffer fusion into something
Like simpleness, order, identity.

I recognize my hands.
By hands used to gardens
The heart fortunately thudding,
Continuous power continuous control
The body's beauty kept continuous,
Is felt for as is thunder,
Palms flat, pressed hard.

Soundlessly gentle, strands of rain
Stroke the stripped ground;
Rain follows rain, quickening.
Spread as they say eagles are,
Stretched as if like rain across air,
But on earth I have made green, familiar,
I arrogate to my embrace
The almost afternoon, praising
Such sequences as this unbreached

Spiral of weather; turning,
It turns: Pinnacled, crystal,
Spindled with prisms, lucent
Under arrowless opened skies,
The towers of air spin off
A glistening morning floss
To thread noon with shimmering.
Drawn
To the upper air the sea
Returns to the sea.
Haze mist downpour; splendid;
I'll be drenched. Gently
Drunk, I think, "In this world
This is the welcome due a citizen."

Under the warm rain I am under
The warm rain makes run together
Earth, its seas and meadows;
Woman, child, crone;
To expect, to remember, to be;
All perfectly separate, all perfect
Known separately; now all seen through
                    One color.
It becomes me where I lie
Gratefully, when I recognize
My glad ghost fixed with surprise
Having learned who cares and why
Color trembles from variety to light

Until as midday strikes I ask
If we are each other's accidents

Structured into the everyday air;
Until like a planet's rings around
A planet and its proper atmosphere
Your afternoon answer makes
A ring around me mapping my
Geography, "Your many and your one
Are to use as you please. My dear.
Like honey the morning sun
Has packed the honeycomb."

I hear and midground midday
Midway in an auspicious midyear
Come full tilt home;
I tell the time, take the glass
Incredulously; hope-
Ridden, I read and see
This birth certificate
Belongs to me.

It says I am of age and a native.
It says I am born free.

INFORMATION

1

Open early to the runes
Of children waking I pace out
The maze of table setting: honey, bread,
Hot milk, butter, loud forks & spoons,
Unmatched cups. The runes reduced & read,
The brilliant mix of voices disperses
As separate embodiments of worlds go out the door.
Expert, I rise, rinse, shelve, restore
Objects to interim order, then sit & pour
Tea from a glossy pot; lucid, as defined
By the cup, it is an oval, circumscribed;
It smells of the smoke of coastal
Hills soft as Southern Sung, gold-shadowing,
In the China of the mind
Only faintly trembling.

2

Rectilinear, the brittle window shapes
For me its landscape version of the world.
Down from a blown March sky rhythms of distance
Intersected by darts of bird
Ripple into a diagonal of rise
Of roof next door and a description
Against the light of oakfact & maplefact.
A cherrybranch tapping the glass
Acts as the groundplane. Dimensions interact
As the line of the wind races through
Composing it, making the composition live.
Mornings, as dozens of seasons have shifted a little
Becoming each other,

I face up to this.
It is informative.

3

I'm lucky; I'm unstruck, not starving; so
I think about what I'm seeing; I abstract
From the crammed nets of rod and cone the catch
My mind takes in for factoring

But when the network breaks with my wanting, sharp,
What is more than rational, to know,
Shorted, I eccentric flow
Sightless into what I see,
Out I go unhanded, feeling for ways of being:
My flecks of blood cool to build the limevein
      pale in the grey stone;
Axons push with the upthrust and downthrust of crabgrass
      climbing the molecular arch of the clawroot, the blade;
      dendrites flower fragile in the seedtassels;
My bones hold it, stressed in steel ceilings;
Borne along unsupported as cloudmist, I lost drift
Exorbitant.

A great recreation
It's nothing remarkable
A flying out a sparkshowering outering and
When searching out persons always one target
      right to the habitless leap of the heart
How contained the stone lies almost still in its changing
How frantic the heat in the sparrow's wingbrain, how subtly

the close structure of feathers like flowerstalks
plumes to be lofty
How at home you move marvelling
where you live looking
for nothing particular
How valuable the tip of your little-used
left ear lobe
How shy we are

GLIDING

Sometimes, riding the thermals, the swallows
drift backward a little at their ease
before they tilt, slide forward down,
and drive their blades of wings stroke on stroke
to catch another column of wind; it lifts
them and they soar. It's a spinning soaring
in the morning windchange; tight
spirals take them to such heights they
vanish; viewed ecstatic, edge-on at their
curve into sheer sky, they turn as
invisible as the principles of flight
            all this time crying
            short crying
—the i's and e's of excellent action—
to say their only
effort is the effort of the act:
sounds we have all sometimes needed,
never made, and seldom deserved
to have a hearer hear.
I look up at them from shade in a walled
well of green among roses and boxwood.
To practice is to take a chance on joy, I think;
the one use of what they do is skill; skill
works against limits to cancel out
sloppiness, tedium, and some pain;
one skill is plenty; taken to the full
is morning swallow-soaring, easily .
voicing the sounds of inner
rejoicing in its readiness.

P.M., MOUNTAIN FLIGHT TERRAIN

To look out from high places without flinching
(I do it belly to the ground) is to suspect how speech
might work, were we ready to face
the drop
into our inner space and find for mind
however awkwardly words and syntax
to negotiate aloud what otherwise
is mystery. It is to suspect our
gravity would change could we surface
the words of that integrating music
we all hear privately.

Hang-gliders haul their gear up here.
They've worked for years to manage a freedom.
They sleep under schema of da Vinci drawings,
keep calculators, wind-tables, equipment catalogues
in the bedside table drawer.
They have passion, brag, argue, share
their dozens of small implements of skill,
their geometry, costumes, support
facilities; train like acrobats,
measure up to standards; are licensed,
play. Clumsy, thick-boned,
beautiful, they practice doing
what they are not suited to;
a second of horror
collects their massy bags of flesh dense
with life and throws them out over
8,000 feet of moving air, as they aim to catch
with the fabric of their thought-up wings their
sustenance. They take flight: people

sail among eagles, as alert,
electric, spending as the mad.
They change the axioms, until
after short soaring,
they home in on a managed
flat of mowed green ground. Sometimes
they can walk back up whole mountains
to their cars, imagining
the next leap into longer independent flight.

Though they'd seem to need wings not hands
to endure the insubstantial field,
having made wings by hand,
they face it readily. It is so huge
it solicits the delight
of those who live open-armed; they
afford it; they enter its emptiness
in a posture of embrace.
Their point of view
would torment others, the hungry,
the cramped and landless, the sad,
who would look through the fields of joy at
the thousand horizontal miles of growing ground
whose juices might, in season,
alleviate their ancient needs.
I'm the ordinary middle of these extremes.

My skill is small and local;
like many ordinary people
I scan the closer mystery: thinking
we want the skill to press against

the limits of our speech, we rehearse
the accents of the inner world, tuneful but
invisible, in hopes the outer ear
will quicken to thought spoken
until
        across the empty air
of personal separateness—and all
are separate—we will sound true or
human to each other,
humankind,
hearing, heard, and
recognized. We elect
readiness to practice this.

Straight ahead of me is sky.
It is wholly flourishing. Below it & me
the earth in its rock-fold distances
is starred by geodes of inhabited villages
where cliff & gorge divert the winds.
Three hundred years ago they snaked a crazy
carriage road over this maritime Alp
just below these heights. Once a woman
kept an inn on it, and help for horses.

The air is ripe. My fists unclench,
and the air, filled with the odor of
thyme & lavender I lie on, fills my hands.
Unshaken by my readiness
or the smallness of my readiness
—or my ignorance of how
the hollows in our speech will fill

as we rehearse aloud against our limits
the names and principled tunes for shapes
and fragrances and absences of shapes
we have in mind—
I envision the next leap, the next
thousand years of practice,
the eventual skill
become like independent flight, habitual.

THE GREAT DEAD,
WHY NOT, MAY KNOW

for Joan Paul, d. April, 1978

No grief goes unrelieved;
some days, half meaning to,
I turn my undefended back
on the grey & snarling scene
of my dissociating pack
and hope.

Some suppose that this post-natal life
where all we have is time, is fetal life,
is where as we bounce and flex in time
our years of moons change us
into beings viable not here
but somewhere attentive. Suppose,
borne down on, we are birthed
into a universe where love's not crazy;
and that split out of time is
death into a medium where
love is the element we cry out to breathe,
big love, general as air here,
specific as breath.

I want to talk to those outlanders
whose perspective I admire;
I listen often to the voices of the dead, and
it feels like my turn in the conversation.
I want to ask, say, Yeats (or
someone else it would make sense to,
Crashaw, Blake, H.D. who
worked out Sappho's honey simile,
Joan word-lover you too, all you

who know what English has to do
with a possible answer)

And I'd say, to set up the question:
Listen,
after over a hundred lifetimes
of summers of honey since Sappho's,
of beekeepers (who set out orchard
rows of nectarplants to bloom
before and after the appletrees,
     who sow alfalfa or tupelo,
     clover or roses,
     "all roses," all summer,
then break the combs out of their dark
and decant the honey heavy & flowery)
—listen, it's no different.
Honey's still dangerous.
Honey's pervasive.
Hunger for honey scalds if satisfied.
I know; I walk around dry-lipped;
my throat burns, and the August air at noon
ices it as I breathe because
I've been eating honey right from the spoon

and (as you, outside observers, can recall)
though petal & pollen nod golden & mild,
honey here burns like gall
and, having burned bitter
     sweet   raw   hot
generates a language for wild
love not limited to pollensoft

couplings of lovers; it generates
the longing to use that language
though there be not any one
to speak it to. Such honey
expressed as if it must be as love
which colors all encounters and lasts
long after one love has gone to seed,
changes the throat of a speaker
till it aches with expectancy
as it asks:

WHAT (as at last I ask
          you of the outland honeyed universe,
          you great dead)
what do you do with love
when it is no more sexual
          than I am sexual,
when it is general
—in me, not mine—
and yet shapes the air,
like breath, like a honeyed
breath of air carrying
meaning between
me and everything there is;
when as if it must it defies
my daily exercise of savagery
and cause for guilt;
when it is absolute,
too sudden to disguise,
unmapped,
unlocalized,

stubbornly addressed
to any eyes—
though it find me no less slothful nor
in any way more kind or wise?

What but
(since the love is in the language)
call it hope
—that helps a little—
and hope to imitate your inlands of example
by praising the possible;
what then but praise the ripening
cure of language which plays
among questions and answers
mediating even love and grief,
what but
     —as the window the morning
       as the foot the tilt of the ground
       as the river the lights of its city—
praise how the actions of language or honey
seem in their transport to express,
from the collected heat and sweetness
of hearing and speaking,
         something
smaller and more human than belief,
some reason to read these thick omens
as good and those outlands as relief.

A NOTE ABOUT THE AUTHOR

Marie Ponsot was born in New York, where she now lives.
She is the translator of thirty-two books, most of them children's
books from the French, and is the author of *True Minds,*
City Lights, Pocket Poets #5, 1957. Among her awards: the
Eunice Tietjens Prize from *Poetry* Magazine and a creative
writing grant from the National Endowment for the Arts. She
has for several years conducted a bimonthly poetry program on
WBAI radio. Marie Ponsot teaches in the Department of
English at Queens College and is the mother of seven children.

A NOTE ON THE TYPE

This book was set on the Linotype in Granjon, a type named
after Robert Granjon. George W. Jones based his designs for
this type upon that used by Claude Garamond (1510–61) in his
beautiful French books. Granjon more closely resembles
Garamond's own type than do the various modern types that
bear his name.

Robert Granjon began his career as type cutter in 1523 and
was one of the first to practice the trade of type founder apart
from that of printer. Between 1557 and 1562 Granjon printed
about twenty books in types designed by himself, following
the cursive handwriting of the time.

Composed by American–Stratford Graphic Services, Inc.,
Brattleboro, Vermont. Printed and bound by American Book–
Stratford Press, Saddle Brook, New Jersey
Designed by Judith Henry